Mastering Qwen2.5-Max

Unlock the Power of

Alibaba's AI

CONTENTS:

Introduction: Understanding Qwen2.5-Max

- Alibaba's Qwen2.5-Max is a cutting-edge AI model that outperforms leading competitors like DeepSeek-V3, OpenAI's GPT-4o, and Meta's Llama 3.1-405B in key AI benchmarks. Powered by a Mixture-of-Experts (MoE) architecture, it offers superior efficiency, knowledge, and reasoning abilities.
- This guide will help developers, businesses, and AI enthusiasts leverage Qwen2.5-Max for tasks like natural language processing (NLP), chatbots, content creation, automation, and enterprise AI solutions.

Chapter 1: What Makes Qwen2.5-Max Unique?

1.1 Mixture-of-Experts (MoE) Efficiency

- Unlike traditional models, Qwen2.5-Max only activates the most relevant "experts" in its network, optimizing performance while reducing computational costs.

1.2 Extensive Pretraining

- Trained on over 20 trillion tokens, ensuring deep contextual understanding.
- Fine-tuned using supervised learning and reinforcement learning from human feedback (RLHF) for high accuracy.

1.3 Benchmark Performance

- Qwen2.5-Max ranks among the best in AI benchmarks:
- Arena-Hard: 89.4, surpassing DeepSeek-V3's 85.5.
- MMLU-Pro: 76.1, slightly ahead of DeepSeek-V3.
- LiveBench: 62.2, leading in real-world AI application tasks.

Chapter 2: How to Access and Use Qwen2.5-Max

2.1 Where to Access It

- Alibaba offers multiple ways to use Qwen2.5-Max:
- Qwen Chat (Web-based platform)
- Alibaba Cloud's Model Studio API (For app integration)

2.2 Setting Up API Access

- Sign up on Alibaba Cloud and navigate to Model Studio.
- Generate API credentials for secure access.
- Integrate with applications using Python, Node.js, or other supported languages.

Chapter 3: Practical Applications of Qwen2.5-Max

3.1 Natural Language Processing (NLP) and Chatbots

- Develop advanced AI assistants for businesses.
- Power multilingual customer support chatbots with real-time translation.

3.2 Content Creation and SEO Optimization

- Generate SEO-optimized blog posts, product descriptions, and ad copy.
- Use AI-powered keyword research and meta descriptions for ranking improvement.

3.3 Automation and Enterprise AI Solutions

- Automate data analysis and business reports.
- Enhance customer experience with AI-driven recommendations.

Chapter 4: Optimizing SEO with Qwen2.5-Max

4.1 AI-Driven Keyword Research

- Use Qwen2.5-Max to generate long-tail keywords and optimize content for search engines.
- Analyze competitor keywords and trends for strategic content planning.

4.2 Writing AI-Powered, SEO-Friendly Content

- Structure articles with engaging headlines, subheadings (H1, H2, H3), and optimized keywords.

- Ensure high readability scores and include meta tags, image alt texts, and internal links.

4.3 Voice Search and Multimodal Optimization

- Optimize content for voice search queries (e.g., "How does Qwen2.5-Max compare to GPT-4o?").
- Leverage Qwen2.5-Max's ability to generate structured data (FAQs, snippets, and JSON-LD) for rich search results.

Conclusion: The Future of AI with Qwen2.5-Max

Mastering Qwen2.5-Max

Unlock the Power of Alibaba's AI

Introduction: Unlocking the Power of Qwen2.5-Max – The Future of AI Innovation

Artificial intelligence is evolving at an unprecedented pace, and Alibaba's **Qwen2.5-Max** stands at the forefront of this transformation. This state-of-the-art AI model has **outperformed leading competitors** such as **DeepSeek-V3, OpenAI's GPT-4o, and Meta's Llama 3.1-405B** in key benchmarks, solidifying its position as a powerhouse in the AI landscape.

With its **Mixture-of-Experts (MoE) architecture**, Qwen2.5-Max delivers unparalleled **efficiency, reasoning capabilities, and deep knowledge**, making it an ideal solution for businesses, developers, and AI enthusiasts looking to integrate cutting-edge AI into their workflows. Whether you need **advanced natural language processing (NLP)**, **intelligent chatbots**,

automated content generation, enterprise AI solutions, or AI-driven automation, Qwen2.5-Max offers a next-level performance that surpasses traditional models.

In this comprehensive guide, we will explore:

✅ **What makes Qwen2.5-Max superior to its competitors**

✅ **How its MoE architecture enhances performance and efficiency**

✅ **Practical applications in various industries, from business automation to creative content**

✅ **How to leverage Qwen2.5-Max for chatbots, NLP, and enterprise AI**

✅ **Best practices for integrating this AI model into your business or development projects**

As AI continues to reshape industries, **staying ahead of the curve** with a model like Qwen2.5-Max can provide a **significant competitive advantage**. Whether you are an AI researcher, developer, entrepreneur, or enterprise leader, this guide will equip you with the insights and strategies needed to maximize the potential of Qwen2.5-Max.

Let's dive in and explore how you can harness this **groundbreaking AI model** to drive **innovation, automation, and business growth** like never before.

Chapter 1:

What Makes Qwen2.5-Max Unique?

As artificial intelligence continues to advance, Alibaba's **Qwen2.5-Max** stands out as a **game-changer in AI development**. This powerful model surpasses competitors like OpenAI's **GPT-4o**, Meta's **Llama 3.1-405B**, and DeepSeek-V3 in several critical areas, offering unmatched **efficiency, scalability, and intelligence**.

In this chapter, we'll explore what makes **Qwen2.5-Max** unique, from its **Mixture-of-Experts (MoE) efficiency** to its **record-breaking benchmark performance**.

1.1 Mixture-of-Experts (MoE) Efficiency

One of the **key innovations** that set **Qwen2.5-Max apart** is its **Mixture-of-Experts (MoE) architecture**. Unlike traditional transformer models that activate all parameters during inference, **MoE selectively activates only the most relevant "experts"** for a given task.

◆ How MoE Works in Qwen2.5-Max

- The model consists of multiple **specialized neural networks** (experts).
- Instead of using all experts for every task, **only the most relevant ones are activated**, optimizing computational efficiency.
- This results in **faster response times** and **lower processing costs**, making Qwen2.5-Max more **scalable** and **resource-efficient** than fully dense models.

✅ Advantages of MoE in Qwen2.5-Max

✓ **Higher Efficiency:** Reduces computational overhead, making large-scale AI applications more cost-effective.

✓ **Superior Adaptability:** Selectively engages experts to improve accuracy across a diverse range of tasks.

✓ **Faster Inference:** Delivers high-speed AI responses without sacrificing quality.

1.2 Extensive Pretraining for Deep Knowledge

To achieve **unmatched accuracy and contextual understanding**, **Qwen2.5-Max** has undergone **extensive pretraining** on a massive **20-trillion-token dataset**—one of the largest in AI history.

◆ **Key Features of Qwen2.5-Max's Training Process**

✓ **Massive Data Exposure:** Pretrained on a diverse dataset covering **scientific research, literature, coding, business, and real-world conversations**.

✓ **Supervised Fine-Tuning:** Carefully refined using **human-annotated datasets** to improve factual   accuracy.

✓ **Reinforcement Learning from Human Feedback (RLHF):** Enhances response quality by incorporating **real-time human evaluations**, making it more **reliable and user-friendly**.

✅ Why This Matters

✓ **More Contextually Aware Responses** – Understands complex prompts with greater accuracy.

✓ **Improved Creativity and Problem-Solving** – Excels in tasks requiring deep reasoning, analysis, and idea generation.

✓ **Better Multilingual Capabilities** – Performs well in multiple languages, making it ideal for global applications.

1.3 Benchmark Performance: Outpacing the Competition

Qwen2.5-Max **dominates AI benchmarks**, proving its **superiority in intelligence, problem-solving, and real-world applications**.

🏛 Key Benchmark Scores

Qwen2.5-Max ranks **among the best AI models**, outpacing DeepSeek-V3 and competing with OpenAI's GPT-4o.

Benchmark	Qwen2.5-Max Score	DeepSeek-V3 Score	Significance
Arena-Hard	89.4	85.5	Excels in advanced reasoning and complex problem-solving.
MMLU-Pro	76.1	75.8	Strong in multi-task learning and general knowledge.
LiveBench	62.2	N/A	Leads in **real-world AI performance**, optimizing practical applications.

✅ Why These Benchmarks Matter

✓ **Arena-Hard:** Tests **advanced reasoning, mathematical abilities, and critical thinking**.

✓ **MMLU-Pro:** Evaluates **multi-task learning**, demonstrating expertise in **science, history, and language understanding**.

✓ **LiveBench:** Measures **real-world AI adaptability**, ensuring Qwen2.5-Max excels in **practical applications** like customer support, automation, and business intelligence.

Conclusion: The Future of AI is Here

With **unparalleled MoE efficiency, deep pretraining, and industry-leading benchmarks**, **Qwen2.5-Max** is not just another AI model—it's a **revolution** in the field of artificial intelligence. Whether you're a **developer, business leader, or AI researcher**, leveraging Qwen2.5-Max can help you **stay ahead of the curve and unlock new possibilities in AI-driven automation, content creation, and enterprise solutions**.

Chapter 2:

How to Access and Use Qwen2.5-Max

Now that we've explored what makes **Qwen2.5-Max** unique, let's dive into **how you can access and start using this cutting-edge AI model**. Alibaba offers several ways to integrate and interact with **Qwen2.5-Max**, making it easier than ever for developers, businesses, and AI enthusiasts to leverage its full potential.

2.1 Where to Access Qwen2.5-Max

Alibaba provides multiple channels for accessing **Qwen2.5-Max**, ensuring flexibility depending on your needs and technical capabilities. Whether you're looking for a **web-based interface** or want to integrate the model into your app, Alibaba has you covered.

◆ Qwen Chat (Web-Based Platform)

Qwen Chat is Alibaba's easy-to-use **web-based platform** that allows you to interact with

Qwen2.5-Max directly through a simple, user-friendly interface. This is ideal for those who want to quickly test the model, generate text, or utilize **Qwen2.5-Max** for natural language processing tasks without complex setup.

Key Features of Qwen Chat:

- **Instant Access:** No installation or technical setup required—simply visit the platform's website.
- **User-Friendly Interface:** Designed to be intuitive, making it easy for anyone to use, from beginners to advanced users.
- **Real-Time Interaction:** Engage in direct conversations or query responses in real-time.
- **Ideal for Testing & Exploration:** Great for exploring the capabilities of **Qwen2.5-Max** for various applications, such as text generation, summarization, and problem-solving.

◆ **Alibaba Cloud's Model Studio API (For App Integration)**

For developers or businesses looking to **integrate Qwen2.5-Max** into their applications or workflows, **Alibaba Cloud's Model Studio API** provides a robust solution. The **Model Studio API** allows you to connect directly with **Qwen2.5-Max**, enabling you to leverage its capabilities in your own systems, apps, or websites.

Key Features of Alibaba Cloud's Model Studio API:

- **Scalable Integration:** Seamlessly integrate **Qwen2.5-Max** into apps, websites, and enterprise solutions.
- **Flexible Usage:** Use the API for **a wide range of tasks**, from chatbots and content generation to data analysis and automation.
- **Customization Options:** Fine-tune the model for specific use cases, enhancing its ability to address your unique business or technical needs.

- **High Performance:** Leverage Alibaba Cloud's infrastructure to ensure that **Qwen2.5-Max** runs smoothly at scale, even for complex or resource-heavy tasks.

2.2 Getting Started with Qwen2.5-Max

1. Sign Up for Access:

- **Qwen Chat:** Simply create an account on the web platform to start interacting with **Qwen2.5-Max**.
- **Model Studio API:** Register for an Alibaba Cloud account and gain access to the **API key** to start integrating **Qwen2.5-Max** into your application.

2. Setting Up Qwen Chat:

- Once signed up, you can begin using the **Qwen Chat** interface to explore various features.
- Simply input a query or task, and the model will generate results in seconds.

Experiment with different prompts to test its capabilities.

3. Integrating via Model Studio API:

- **API Documentation:** Refer to the provided documentation for detailed setup instructions, including how to authenticate with your **API key**.
- **Test Integration:** Start by testing basic API calls to generate responses or perform tasks like **text summarization** or **content generation**.
- **Scale and Customize:** Once familiar with the API, you can scale your integration or fine-tune the model for more specialized use cases.

2.3 Benefits of Accessing Qwen2.5-Max

No matter how you choose to access **Qwen2.5-Max**, there are clear benefits for both developers and businesses.

✅ For Developers:

- **Simple API Setup:** Alibaba Cloud provides clear and detailed documentation, making it easy to integrate the **Qwen2.5-Max API** into your projects.
- **Advanced AI Capabilities:** Build intelligent applications powered by one of the most **advanced AI models** available, improving user experiences and automating tasks.
- **Scalability:** Easily scale your usage based on your needs, from small experiments to enterprise-level integrations.

✅ For Businesses:

- **Cost-Effective:** Alibaba's platform allows for **flexible pricing**, ensuring that businesses can access AI capabilities according to their budget.
- **Real-Time Insights:** Use **Qwen2.5-Max** to provide instant responses, enabling real-time customer support or business intelligence.

- **Competitive Edge:** By integrating **Qwen2.5-Max**, you gain access to an AI model that outperforms competitors, ensuring your business stays ahead of the curve.

Accessing Qwen2.5-Max through either **Qwen Chat** or the **Alibaba Cloud Model Studio API** provides flexible options for users with varying needs, from casual exploration to enterprise-grade integration. Whether you're a developer, business leader, or AI enthusiast, **Qwen2.5-Max** offers an accessible and powerful tool for **transforming your AI-driven projects**.

2.2 Setting Up API Access

To fully leverage **Qwen2.5-Max** for your applications, you need to set up API access through **Alibaba Cloud's Model Studio**. Below is a **step-by-step guide** on how to get started with

API access, ensuring a smooth integration into your projects.

1. Sign Up on Alibaba Cloud and Navigate to Model Studio

Before you can use the **Qwen2.5-Max API**, you'll need to create an account on **Alibaba Cloud**. Follow these steps:

- **Create an Alibaba Cloud Account:** Visit Alibaba Cloud and sign up for a free account if you don't have one yet. This will give you access to the platform and its services.
- **Navigate to Model Studio:** Once your account is set up, go to the **Model Studio** section on the Alibaba Cloud console. Model Studio is where you can access **Qwen2.5-Max** and other AI models offered by Alibaba Cloud.

2. Generate API Credentials for Secure Access

After logging into **Model Studio**, the next step is to generate **API credentials**. These credentials allow you to securely connect to the **Qwen2.5-Max API** and start utilizing its capabilities within your applications. Here's how to generate them:

- **Access the API Management Console:** In **Model Studio**, look for the API management section, where you can create and manage your credentials.

- **Create API Keys:** Generate your **API key** and **secret key**. These are essential for authenticating your API requests. Be sure to keep them secure and never expose them publicly.

- **Set Permissions:** Depending on your use case, you can customize the permissions for your API keys to control which operations are allowed when interacting with **Qwen2.5-Max**.

3. Integrate with Applications Using Python, Node.js, or Other Supported Languages

With your **API credentials** in hand, the next step is integrating **Qwen2.5-Max** into your application. Alibaba Cloud supports multiple programming languages for API integration, including **Python**, **Node.js**, and others. Here's a high-level overview of the integration process:

- **Choose Your Language:** Select the programming language you are most comfortable with or the one that best suits your application. Alibaba provides SDKs and examples for **Python**, **Node.js**, **Java**, and more.

- **Install the SDK or Library:** Use the provided SDK or install relevant libraries to interact with the API. For example, if you're using **Python**, you might install the SDK via pip:

bash
CopierModifier
pip install alibaba-cloud-sdk

- **Authenticate API Requests:** In your code, authenticate using the **API key** and **secret key**. Here's an example of how this might look in **Python**:

```python
CopierModifier
from alibaba_cloud_sdk import AlibabaCloud

# Initialize the API client with your credentials
client = AlibabaCloud(api_key='your_api_key', secret_key='your_secret_key')

# Make API requests
response = client.call('Qwen2.5-Max', 'generate_text', prompt='Your query')
print(response)
```

- **Test and Scale:** Test the integration with simple API calls. Once confirmed, you can scale your integration to suit more complex use cases like **chatbot integration**, **content generation**, and **automation** tasks.

Conclusion

Setting up **API access** for **Qwen2.5-Max** on **Alibaba Cloud** is straightforward, whether you're working with Python, Node.js, or another language. Once you've completed the setup, you'll be able to integrate **Qwen2.5-Max** into your applications, automating processes, enhancing content creation, and unlocking the true power of this advanced AI model.

In the next section, we'll explore **optimizing API usage** to get the most out of **Qwen2.5-Max**, including best practices for scaling and fine-tuning. Stay tuned for more insights!

Chapter 3:

Practical Applications of Qwen2.5-Max

In this chapter, we will explore the practical applications of **Qwen2.5-Max** and how its advanced capabilities can be leveraged across a wide range of use cases. From **natural language processing (NLP)** to **AI-driven chatbots**, **Qwen2.5-Max** offers powerful solutions for modern businesses and developers.

3.1 Natural Language Processing (NLP) and Chatbots

Natural Language Processing (NLP) is one of the most significant advancements in AI, enabling machines to understand, interpret, and generate human language. **Qwen2.5-Max**, with its deep understanding of language and context, excels in a variety of NLP tasks, making it a top choice for building intelligent chatbots and other language-related applications.

◆ Develop Advanced AI Assistants for Businesses

With **Qwen2.5-Max**, businesses can create **advanced AI assistants** capable of understanding and responding to customer queries in real-time. These assistants can be deployed across various channels, including websites, mobile apps, and social media platforms, improving customer interaction and satisfaction.

Benefits of AI Assistants with Qwen2.5-Max:

- **Contextual Understanding:** Thanks to its extensive pretraining on over 20 trillion tokens, **Qwen2.5-Max** can engage in meaningful conversations, recognizing context, tone, and intent, which enhances the accuracy and relevance of responses.

- **Real-Time Response Generation:** Whether it's answering frequently asked questions or handling complex customer inquiries, the AI assistant can provide instant responses, ensuring customers receive the support they need without delays.

- **Enhanced User Experience:** Personalized responses based on past interactions and user preferences ensure customers feel valued, leading to improved engagement and satisfaction.

- **Business Process Automation:** Automate routine customer service tasks such as handling queries, troubleshooting common issues, and providing product recommendations, freeing up your human agents to focus on more complex tasks.

Example Use Cases for AI Assistants:

- **E-commerce:** Guide customers through the shopping process, provide personalized recommendations, and assist with order tracking.

- **Healthcare:** Help patients schedule appointments, answer medical inquiries, and provide wellness tips.

- **Finance:** Assist with balance inquiries, transaction processing, and offering financial advice.

◆ **Power Multilingual Customer Support Chatbots with Real-Time Translation**

In today's globalized world, providing **multilingual customer support** is essential for businesses looking to engage with international audiences. **Qwen2.5-Max**'s advanced **multilingual NLP capabilities** make it a perfect solution for powering **real-time translation** in customer support chatbots.

Benefits of Multilingual Chatbots with Qwen2.5-Max:

- **Real-Time Translation:** With its powerful multilingual processing capabilities, **Qwen2.5-Max** can translate text between various languages in real-time, breaking down language barriers and enabling smooth communication with customers from around the world.

- **Contextual Translation:** Unlike basic translation tools, **Qwen2.5-Max** ensures that translations maintain the context and meaning of the original text, providing more accurate and natural-sounding responses in the target language.

- **Seamless Multilingual Support:** Whether you're providing customer service in **English, Spanish, French, Chinese**, or any other language, **Qwen2.5-Max** can handle multiple languages simultaneously, improving accessibility for diverse customer bases.

- **Cost-Effective Solution:** By automating multilingual support, businesses can reduce the need for hiring agents who speak multiple languages, saving on operational costs while still delivering high-quality support.

Example Use Cases for Multilingual Chatbots:

- **Retail:** Support customers in different languages on your website or in-app support chat.
- **Travel and Hospitality:** Help international travelers with booking assistance, flight information, and travel recommendations in their native language.
- **Customer Service:** Enable customer service teams to assist customers across borders without the need for a dedicated team in each region.

3.2 Other NLP Applications

Beyond chatbots, **Qwen2.5-Max** can be utilized for various other **NLP applications**, including:

- **Text Summarization:** Automatically condense long documents or articles into shorter, more digestible summaries, making it easier for users to quickly grasp key points.

- **Sentiment Analysis:** Analyze customer reviews, social media posts, or feedback to determine customer sentiment and tailor marketing or customer support strategies accordingly.

- **Speech Recognition:** Integrate **Qwen2.5-Max** into voice-enabled applications to transcribe speech into text and provide accurate voice interactions.

3.3 Conclusion

With its cutting-edge **NLP capabilities** and **real-time translation features**, **Qwen2.5-Max** opens up new opportunities for businesses and developers to create **intelligent AI-driven applications** that enhance customer experiences and streamline operations. Whether you're developing a **customer support chatbot**, building a **global e-commerce platform**, or automating internal processes, **Qwen2.5-Max** offers the tools and performance needed to stay ahead in today's competitive landscape.

3.2 Content Creation and SEO Optimization

Qwen2.5-Max isn't just a tool for advanced **natural language processing (NLP)** and **chatbots**. Its powerful language generation capabilities make it an exceptional choice for **content creation** and **SEO optimization**. From writing blog posts to generating ad copy, **Qwen2.5-Max** can streamline your content workflows while ensuring your content ranks higher in search engine results.

◆ **Generate SEO-Optimized Blog Posts, Product Descriptions, and Ad Copy**

One of the standout features of **Qwen2.5-Max** is its ability to generate high-quality, **SEO-optimized content** in a fraction of the time it would take a human writer. Whether you need blog posts, product descriptions, or compelling ad copy, **Qwen2.5-Max** can produce content that is not only engaging but also designed to perform well on search engines.

Benefits of Using Qwen2.5-Max for Content Creation:

- **Consistent Quality: Qwen2.5-Max** is trained on vast amounts of data, ensuring that the content it generates is coherent, accurate, and relevant to the target audience.
- **Adaptable Tone and Style:** Whether you need professional, casual, or conversational content, **Qwen2.5-Max** can adjust its writing style to match your brand's voice.
- **Time Efficiency:** By automating the content creation process, **Qwen2.5-Max** allows businesses to produce large volumes of content in a short amount of time, which is particularly beneficial for high-demand environments like e-commerce or marketing agencies.

Example Use Cases for Content Creation:

- **Blog Posts:** Generate informative blog posts around trending topics or industry-specific keywords, designed to attract organic traffic and engage your audience.
- **Product Descriptions:** Write compelling, SEO-friendly product descriptions that highlight key features, benefits, and specifications, encouraging both search engines and customers to take action.
- **Ad Copy:** Craft engaging ad copy for Google Ads, social media campaigns, or landing pages that resonates with potential customers and increases conversion rates.

◆ Use AI-Powered Keyword Research and Meta Descriptions for Ranking Improvement

SEO isn't just about creating great content—it's also about making sure that content is **optimized for search engines**. **Qwen2.5-Max** goes beyond basic content generation and can help improve your SEO strategy through **AI-powered keyword research** and **meta descriptions**.

Benefits of AI-Powered SEO Optimization:

- **Keyword Research: Qwen2.5-Max** can suggest relevant keywords based on your content topic, helping you target high-traffic, low-competition search terms. It analyzes search trends and user behavior, ensuring the keywords it generates are highly relevant to your target audience.

- **Keyword Placement: Qwen2.5-Max** can generate content with optimal keyword placement, ensuring that keywords are naturally incorporated throughout the text without keyword stuffing, which improves readability and ranking.

- **Meta Descriptions:** The model can craft SEO-friendly **meta descriptions** that succinctly summarize the content, while incorporating primary keywords to improve click-through rates from search engine results pages (SERPs).

- **Content Structure: Qwen2.5-Max** can recommend or generate appropriate headers (H1, H2, H3, etc.) to organize the content and make it more accessible for both users and search engines. A well-structured content layout can boost your SEO ranking and help improve user engagement.

Example Use Cases for SEO Optimization:

- **Blog Posts:** Generate blog posts with optimized keywords, engaging meta descriptions, and appropriate internal linking to drive organic traffic.
- **Product Pages:** Create optimized product pages that rank for specific keywords related to your products, boosting visibility and sales.
- **Landing Pages:** Write landing page content that is both conversion-focused and optimized for search engines, ensuring it ranks while driving leads and conversions.

By utilizing **Qwen2.5-Max** for **content creation** and **SEO optimization**, businesses can dramatically improve their content strategy, ensuring they not only create valuable and engaging content but also increase their chances of ranking higher on search engines. With its advanced capabilities in **keyword research, meta descriptions**, and **content generation**, **Qwen2.5-Max** is an indispensable tool for businesses looking to enhance their online presence and drive organic traffic.

3.3 Automation and Enterprise AI Solutions

In today's fast-paced business environment, efficiency and scalability are paramount. **Qwen2.5-Max** can play a pivotal role in **automating business processes** and providing **enterprise-level AI solutions** that drive productivity and innovation. From automating **data analysis** to enhancing customer experience through **AI-driven recommendations, Qwen2.5-**

Max offers robust capabilities that transform enterprise operations.

◆ Automate Data Analysis and Business Reports

One of the most time-consuming tasks for businesses is analyzing large volumes of data and generating insightful reports. **Qwen2.5-Max** simplifies this process by automating **data analysis**, enabling companies to make data-driven decisions quickly and effectively.

Benefits of Automating Data Analysis with Qwen2.5-Max:

- **Speed and Efficiency: Qwen2.5-Max** processes large datasets in record time, enabling businesses to obtain insights from their data without manual intervention. This can significantly reduce operational bottlenecks and improve decision-making.
- **Actionable Insights: Qwen2.5-Max** doesn't just analyze data—it also provides actionable insights. By identifying trends,

patterns, and correlations, the model can help businesses make more informed decisions, improve forecasting, and identify new opportunities.

- **Custom Reporting:** Whether you need financial reports, performance metrics, or customer analytics, **Qwen2.5-Max** can automate the creation of **customized reports**, ensuring they are tailored to your business's unique needs. These reports can be generated at regular intervals and can include visualizations, saving time and resources.

- **Predictive Analytics:** By integrating **Qwen2.5-Max** with your data systems, businesses can leverage **predictive analytics** to anticipate trends and outcomes. This is especially useful for inventory management, customer behavior analysis, and market trend forecasting.

Example Use Cases for Data Analysis Automation:

- **Financial Reporting:** Automate the generation of monthly, quarterly, or yearly financial reports, allowing accounting and finance teams to focus on strategic planning rather than data entry and analysis.
- **Sales Performance Analysis:** Generate sales performance reports, analyze customer behavior, and predict future sales trends to help businesses optimize their sales strategy.
- **Customer Insights:** Analyze customer data to identify preferences, purchasing patterns, and demographics, enabling businesses to better tailor their products and marketing strategies.

◆ Enhance Customer Experience with AI-Driven Recommendations

In today's competitive landscape, delivering a personalized customer experience is essential for business success. **Qwen2.5-Max** can enhance customer engagement by providing **AI-driven recommendations** based on user behavior, preferences, and historical data.

Benefits of AI-Driven Recommendations with Qwen2.5-Max:

- **Personalized Experiences: Qwen2.5-Max** uses its advanced AI capabilities to analyze customer data and generate personalized recommendations for products, services, or content. This helps businesses deliver relevant and engaging experiences to their customers, driving loyalty and increasing sales.

- **Real-Time Recommendations:** With its ability to process data in real time, **Qwen2.5-Max** can offer **instant recommendations** to customers, whether they're shopping on an e-commerce site, browsing content, or interacting with a chatbot.

- **Cross-Selling and Upselling:** By understanding customer behavior and preferences, **Qwen2.5-Max** can suggest complementary products (cross-selling) or higher-end alternatives (upselling), helping businesses increase their average order value and revenue.

- **Improved Conversion Rates:** Personalized recommendations can significantly boost conversion rates by guiding customers to products or services they are most likely to purchase, thereby improving overall business performance.

Example Use Cases for AI-Driven Recommendations:

- **E-Commerce:** Recommend products based on past purchases, browsing history, and user preferences to increase customer engagement and sales.

- **Media and Entertainment:** Suggest movies, music, or shows based on user preferences and viewing history, enhancing customer retention and satisfaction.

- **Online Learning Platforms:** Provide personalized course recommendations based on the learner's past activities, progress, and interests.

3.4 Conclusion

By automating key business processes like **data analysis** and enhancing the customer experience with **AI-driven recommendations**, **Qwen2.5-Max** empowers businesses to scale operations, improve decision-making, and drive revenue growth. Whether you're automating complex reporting tasks or personalizing product offerings, **Qwen2.5-Max** provides the tools necessary to streamline operations and create smarter, more efficient workflows.

Chapter 4:

Optimizing SEO with Qwen2.5-Max

In the ever-evolving world of SEO, staying ahead of the competition requires innovative strategies. **Qwen2.5-Max** offers powerful tools to optimize SEO efforts, particularly through **AI-driven keyword research**. With its advanced **natural language processing** capabilities, **Qwen2.5-Max** can help you generate highly effective **long-tail keywords**, analyze **competitor keywords**, and leverage **SEO trends** to boost your content's visibility and ranking.

4.1 AI-Driven Keyword Research

Effective **keyword research** is the foundation of any successful SEO strategy. With **Qwen2.5-Max**, businesses can automate and enhance this process, ensuring that they target the most relevant and high-performing keywords for their content. **Qwen2.5-Max** not only simplifies traditional keyword research but also provides deep insights into search intent, competition, and trending keywords, giving your content a significant edge in search engine rankings.

◆ Generate Long-Tail Keywords and Optimize Content for Search Engines

Long-tail keywords—specific, longer phrases that are less competitive but highly targeted—are key to ranking well in search engines, especially for businesses looking to attract a more niche audience. **Qwen2.5-Max** can generate these long-tail keywords by analyzing current trends, search behaviors, and user intent.

Benefits of Using Qwen2.5-Max for Long-Tail Keyword Generation:

- **Improved Search Intent Matching:** **Qwen2.5-Max** excels at identifying the true intent behind search queries. It helps generate long-tail keywords that align closely with what users are actually looking for, improving your chances of ranking for high-intent searches.

- **Target Niche Audiences:** By targeting specific and less competitive long-tail keywords, **Qwen2.5-Max** helps businesses attract more relevant visitors who are looking for precise solutions or information.
- **Increased Conversion Rates:** Long-tail keywords typically result in higher conversion rates since they reflect a more specific search query, often coming from users closer to making a purchasing decision or engaging with the content.

Example Use Cases for Long-Tail Keyword Generation:

- **Blog Content:** Use **Qwen2.5-Max** to generate long-tail keywords around niche topics or frequently asked questions in your industry, which can help you rank for highly relevant searches with lower competition.
- **Product Pages:** Target long-tail keywords for product descriptions that reflect what customers are specifically searching for

(e.g., "best organic skincare products for sensitive skin").

- **Service Pages:** Tailor service-related keywords to niche needs, such as "affordable home renovation contractors in [city]" or "best pet-friendly hotels near [location]."

◆ Analyze Competitor Keywords and Trends for Strategic Content Planning

Another powerful application of **Qwen2.5-Max** is its ability to analyze **competitor keywords** and uncover trends within your industry. **Qwen2.5-Max** can process competitor data, search trends, and real-time SEO metrics to help you understand what is working for your competitors, and how you can leverage these insights to craft a stronger SEO strategy.

Benefits of Competitor Analysis with Qwen2.5-Max:

- **Identify Content Gaps:** By analyzing the keywords your competitors are ranking for,

Qwen2.5-Max helps you uncover opportunities for content that they may have overlooked. This allows you to target untapped keyword spaces and build content that addresses user needs more effectively.

- **Track SEO Trends: Qwen2.5-Max** can identify emerging trends in your industry or vertical, ensuring you are ahead of the curve when it comes to keyword targeting. By using these trends, you can create content that aligns with current search demands, improving your chances of ranking higher.

- **Competitive Advantage:** Gaining insights into competitor keyword strategies allows you to make data-driven decisions about where to allocate your SEO resources, ensuring that you target the most valuable keywords and avoid unnecessary competition.

Example Use Cases for Competitor Keyword and Trend Analysis:

- **Content Strategy Development:** Use **Qwen2.5-Max** to identify content topics and keywords that competitors are ranking for, and build superior content around those keywords to gain an edge.
- **Backlink Strategy:** Analyze competitor backlink profiles to identify potential sites to target for guest posts or partnerships.
- **SEO Campaign Optimization:** Monitor keyword shifts and trends to adapt your SEO campaign, ensuring you are targeting the most relevant terms.

4.2 Conclusion

Qwen2.5-Max revolutionizes the traditional process of **keyword research** by leveraging AI to generate **long-tail keywords**, analyze **competitor strategies**, and uncover **emerging trends**. By integrating **Qwen2.5-Max** into your SEO workflow, you can ensure your content is always optimized for the right keywords, driving more organic traffic and improving your search engine rankings.

4.2 Writing AI-Powered, SEO-Friendly Content

Crafting SEO-optimized content is a critical part of any successful digital marketing strategy. With **Qwen2.5-Max**, writing **AI-powered, SEO-friendly content** has never been easier. This section covers how to leverage **Qwen2.5-Max** to create engaging, keyword-optimized articles that both rank well on search engines and engage readers.

◆ Structure Articles with Engaging Headlines, Subheadings (H1, H2, H3), and Optimized Keywords

Effective content structure plays a significant role in SEO success. **Qwen2.5-Max** helps you create well-structured articles that adhere to SEO best practices, including proper use of **headlines (H1, H2, H3)**, **optimized keywords**, and **engaging**

subheadings that encourage both readability and search engine optimization.

Why is Article Structure Important for SEO?

- **User Experience:** Proper use of headings and subheadings makes your content easier to scan, improving user engagement. Visitors are more likely to stay on your page if they can quickly find the information they're looking for.
- **Keyword Relevance:** Search engines value articles that use keywords strategically. **Qwen2.5-Max** assists in determining the most effective places to place primary and secondary keywords within your headings and subheadings, boosting content relevance and improving your rankings.
- **Content Hierarchy:** Search engines favor a clear content hierarchy, which is achieved through appropriate use of H1, H2, and H3 tags. **Qwen2.5-Max** can help structure your content to ensure it's both easy to follow and optimized for SEO.

Example: If you're writing an article about "The Benefits of Remote Work," **Qwen2.5-Max** would recommend structuring your article with an **H1** for the main title, **H2** for primary sections (e.g., "What is Remote Work?"), and **H3** for subsections (e.g., "Advantages for Employers" or "Impact on Employee Productivity"). You can strategically insert **long-tail keywords** like "benefits of remote work in 2025" into these headings for improved ranking.

◆ Ensure High Readability Scores

For both SEO and user experience, ensuring your content is readable is crucial. **Qwen2.5-Max** excels at helping you write articles that maintain high readability scores, which not only improve user engagement but also favor better rankings on search engines.

Key Factors for High Readability:

- **Concise Sentences:** Avoiding overly complex sentences helps readers quickly digest the content.

- **Simple Vocabulary:** Use clear and simple language to make your content accessible to a wider audience.

- **Short Paragraphs:** Short, digestible paragraphs make your content more user-friendly, increasing the likelihood of readers staying on your page longer.

How Qwen2.5-Max Enhances Readability:

- **Sentence Structure Optimization:** **Qwen2.5-Max** can suggest improvements to sentence structure, ensuring your content flows naturally and is easy to follow.

- **Content Personalization:** Whether you're writing for an **industry-specific** or **general** audience, **Qwen2.5-Max** can adapt the tone and complexity of the content based on the target audience's needs.

- **Real-Time Readability Feedback:** As you write, **Qwen2.5-Max** can provide real-time feedback, suggesting edits to improve sentence clarity, active voice usage, and overall readability.

◆ Include Meta Tags, Image Alt Texts, and Internal Links

On-page SEO goes beyond just keyword optimization. **Qwen2.5-Max** ensures that your content is fully optimized by assisting in the creation of essential elements like **meta tags**, **image alt texts**, and **internal links**. These elements significantly impact both SEO rankings and user experience.

◆ Meta Tags

Meta tags, including **meta titles** and **meta descriptions**, provide search engines with a summary of your content. **Qwen2.5-Max** can help generate **SEO-optimized meta titles** and **meta descriptions** that are concise, relevant, and contain target keywords.

- **Meta Title Example:** "The Benefits of Remote Work in 2025 | Why Remote Work is Here to Stay"
- **Meta Description Example:** "Discover the benefits of remote work in 2025, including enhanced productivity, work-life balance, and cost savings for employers. Learn why remote work is the future."

◆ **Image Alt Texts**

Search engines cannot "see" images, but they can read **image alt text**. **Qwen2.5-Max** helps you generate **descriptive and SEO-friendly alt texts** for images that improve both your content's accessibility and SEO ranking.

- **Example Alt Text:** "Remote employee working from home office on laptop, representing the rise of remote work in 2025."

◆ Internal Links

Internal links are essential for improving site navigation, distributing page authority across your website, and keeping users engaged. **Qwen2.5-Max** can suggest relevant **internal links** to enhance your content's structure, helping users easily navigate to related articles.

Example of Internal Linking: In an article on remote work, you could link to other relevant pieces like "How to Set Up a Home Office for Remote Work" or "Top Tools for Effective Remote Team Collaboration."

4.3 Conclusion

Writing **AI-powered, SEO-friendly content** with **Qwen2.5-Max** simplifies the process of crafting high-quality articles that both rank well on search engines and engage readers. By optimizing content structure, readability, meta tags, image alt texts, and internal links, **Qwen2.5-Max** helps you create content that not only attracts traffic but also keeps visitors on your page longer, improving both SEO and user experience.

4.3 Voice Search and Multimodal Optimization

With the rise of voice assistants like Siri, Alexa, and Google Assistant, optimizing content for **voice search** has become essential for staying ahead in SEO. Voice search queries are typically longer and more conversational, requiring different strategies compared to traditional text-based searches. **Qwen2.5-Max** is uniquely equipped to help you optimize your content for **voice search** and enhance **multimodal search results**.

◆ Optimize Content for Voice Search Queries

Voice search queries tend to be more natural and question-based, as users speak conversationally instead of typing brief keywords. **Qwen2.5-Max** can assist in optimizing content to cater to these natural language patterns.

Voice Search Query Characteristics:

- **Long-Tail Keywords:** Voice searches often use **long-tail keywords** that are longer, more detailed, and conversational.
- **Question Formats:** Queries are typically phrased in the form of questions, such as "What are the benefits of remote work in 2025?" or "How does Qwen2.5-Max compare to GPT-4o?"
- **Local Intent:** Many voice searches are location-specific, asking for directions or local services, like "Where is the nearest coffee shop?"

How to Optimize Content for Voice Search with Qwen2.5-Max:

- **Use Conversational Keywords:** Since voice search queries are naturally more conversational, **Qwen2.5-Max** can help you identify and incorporate long-tail keywords that reflect spoken language.

Example:

Instead of targeting "remote work benefits," you might optimize for queries like:

- "What are the top benefits of remote work in 2025?"
- "Why should businesses adopt remote work?"

- **Answer Questions Clearly:** Search engines often pull content that directly answers user questions for **featured snippets**. **Qwen2.5-Max** can assist in crafting clear, concise answers to frequently asked questions.

Example   **Answer:**

"Qwen2.5-Max outperforms GPT-4o due to its Mixture-of-Experts architecture, which optimizes computational efficiency while delivering exceptional performance across key benchmarks."

- **Natural Language Processing (NLP):** With **Qwen2.5-Max's NLP capabilities**, you can better understand and optimize your

60

content to mirror how people naturally speak when using voice search.

◆ Leverage Qwen2.5-Max's Ability to Generate Structured Data

Structured data is key to enhancing your visibility in search engines, especially for rich search results like **FAQ snippets**, **knowledge panels**, and **Google's Featured Snippets**. **Qwen2.5-Max** can generate structured data in formats like **JSON-LD**, **FAQ schemas**, and other rich snippets that provide search engines with context about your content.

Types of Structured Data to Optimize:

- **FAQs:** Generate a structured FAQ section for your content to improve the likelihood of being featured in Google's FAQ snippets.

Example FAQ Schema:

```json
{
  "@context": "https://schema.org",
  "@type": "FAQPage",
  "mainEntity": [{
    "@type": "Question",
    "name": "How does Qwen2.5-Max compare to GPT-4o?",
    "acceptedAnswer": {
      "@type": "Answer",
      "text": "Qwen2.5-Max outperforms GPT-4o by utilizing Mixture-of-Experts (MoE) architecture, making it more efficient and powerful across key benchmarks."
    }
  }]
}
```

- **Rich Snippets:** Enhance your content with **structured data** for articles, reviews, and product pages to increase the likelihood of appearing in rich snippets. This can help users find your content directly through search engine results, increasing click-through rates (CTR).

- **JSON-LD (Linked Data): Qwen2.5-Max** can generate **JSON-LD structured data** to provide search engines with detailed information about your content, making it easier for them to display your content as rich search results.

Example JSON-LD for a product page:

json

```json
{
  "@context": "https://schema.org",
  "@type": "Product",
  "name": "Qwen2.5-Max AI Model",
  "description": "Qwen2.5-Max is a cutting-edge AI model designed for high efficiency and powerful reasoning abilities.",
  "brand": "Alibaba",
  "url": "https://example.com/qwen2-5-max",
```

```
"image":
"https://example.com/images/qwen2-5-
max.jpg"
}
```

By implementing **structured data** and optimizing for **voice search queries**, **Qwen2.5-Max** enhances your content's visibility in search engine results, helping you reach more users through both traditional and voice search methods.

Optimizing content for **voice search** and **multimodal search results** is no longer optional—it's essential for staying competitive in the evolving landscape of SEO. With **Qwen2.5-Max**'s advanced capabilities, you can create content that is not only optimized for traditional search engines but also designed to capture the growing trend of voice search.

Conclusion:

The Future of AI with Qwen2.5-Max

Alibaba's **Qwen2.5-Max** is undoubtedly a game-changer in the AI space, offering groundbreaking innovations that propel the industry forward. By leveraging its **Mixture-of-Experts (MoE)** architecture, **Qwen2.5-Max** enhances **efficiency**, **accuracy**, and **cost-effectiveness**—making it a powerful tool for **businesses**, **developers**, and **content creators** alike.

From **chatbots** that offer sophisticated, human-like interactions to **automation** solutions that streamline workflows, **Qwen2.5-Max** is revolutionizing how tasks are completed in the digital landscape. Whether you're crafting **SEO-optimized content** or building **enterprise AI solutions**, this AI model equips you with the tools to excel in an increasingly competitive market.

Key Takeaways:

- **Versatile Applications:** Whether in natural language processing (NLP), **SEO optimization**, or **automation, Qwen2.5-Max** provides versatile solutions for diverse needs.

- **Enhanced Productivity: Qwen2.5-Max** maximizes **efficiency** and **accuracy**, helping businesses reduce operational costs while improving performance.

- **AI-Driven Innovation:** Businesses, developers, and content creators can stay ahead of the curve by adopting **Qwen2.5-Max** as their go-to AI solution in this **AI-driven digital age**.

As AI continues to evolve, **Qwen2.5-Max** stands as a leader in this transformation, ready to shape the future of AI-powered solutions and help enterprises thrive in the digital world. Embrace the power of **Qwen2.5-Max** and unlock new possibilities for your business.

Table of Contents

www.ingramcontent.com/pod-product-compliance
Lightning Source LLC
LaVergne TN
LVHW052321060326
832902LV00023B/4523